The ETHERINGTON BROTHERS' Long Gone DON

The TERROR-COTTA ARMY

LONG GONE DON: THE TERROR-COTTA ARMY
is a
DAVID FICKLING BOOK

First published in Great Britain in 2017 by
David Fickling Books,
31 Beaumont Street, Oxford, OX1 2NP

www.davidficklingbooks.com

Text copyright © Robin Etherington, 2017
Illustrations copyright © Lorenzo Etherington, 2017

978-1-910989-78-4

DAVID FICKLING BOOKS Reg. No. 8340307

A CIP catalogue record for this book is available from the British Library.

Printed and bound in Great Britain by Sterling

Papers used by David Fickling Books are from
well-managed forests and other responsible sources.

This book is dedicated to...
"Mimi and CJ – with my eternal
thanks for providing all the comedy
inspiration I could ever need!"
- Robin

"Esther, the sparkling centre of
my entire world."
- Lorenzo

THE REMARKABLE TALE OF **DON SKELTON** BEGINS AT THE VERY END.

FORTUNA *JUNIOR SCHOOL* PROVIDED THE STAGE FOR THE FINAL ACT OF DON'S LIFE, WHERE HE MET A STICKY END.

A BADLY ROLLED DICE TRIPPED UP THE DINNER LADY, WHO DROPPED A PAN OF CUSTARD THAT LANDED ON EDDIE'S *BACK*...

EDDIE JUMPED IN SURPRISE AND FLUNG A PLAYING CARD, KNOCKING OPEN THE CAGE DOOR TO PAULA'S *HAMSTER*...

THE HAMSTER RAN UP THE CARETAKER'S *TROUSER LEG.* HE FELL OFF HIS LADDER AND LANDED IN A PILE OF *SICK* (CREATED BY BOB, A POORLY FIRST YEAR)...

AND PAULA, BELIEVING THE SICK-COVERED CARETAKER TO BE A *GHOST*, BACKED INTO THE *LADDER*, WHICH FELL ONTO DON'S HEAD, KNOCKING HIM OUT COLD!

AND SO IT WAS THAT POOR DON DROWNED IN A BOWL OF OXTAIL SOUP. YES, HIS FATE WAS A STRANGE ONE ... BUT FATE WAS NOT YET FINISHED!

FOR THAT WAS WHEN EVENTS TOOK AN EVEN *STRANGER* TURN...

DON FELL, *LITERALLY*, INTO AN UNDERWORLD. A STRANGE, MYSTERIOUS AND OFTEN TERRIFYING PLACE KNOWN AS **BROILERDOOM!** IT IS HERE, IN THE HEART OF **CORPSE CITY,** SURROUNDED AND HOUNDED BY MISFITS AND MONSTERS, THAT DON HAS FOUND A NEW HOME...

AAARGH!

DON SKELTON

DON *MIGHT* BE DEAD, BUT THAT HASN'T STOPPED HIM FROM HAVING ADVENTURES! HE REMAINS DETERMINED TO FIND HIS WAY HOME!

CASTANET

DON'S BEST FRIEND AND GUIDE! THE ONE THING HARDER THAN BEING A TINY CROW IN A CITY OF GIANT MONSTERS IS KEEPING DON OUT OF TROUBLE!

LEWD

LEWD OWNS *THE DEMON DRINK,* DON'S TEMPORARY HOME. HE IS GOOD AT THREE THINGS: SHOUTING, FIGHTING ... AND MORE FIGHTING!

SAFINA

SAFINA IS THE GREATEST THIEF THE CITY HAS EVER KNOWN! HER TALENTS HAVE SAVED DON'S LIFE MORE THAN ONCE.

SPODE

SPODE IS THE DEMON IN CHARGE OF CORPSE CITY AND HE IS ALSO DON'S SWORN ENEMY! AS ENEMIES GO, THAT IS *BAD* NEWS...

THANATOS

MANY STRANGE CREATURES LIVE IN THE UNDERWORLD, BUT ONLY ONE IS BELIEVED TO HAVE A SECRET PORTAL IN HIS TUMMY THAT COULD SEND DON HOME!

WELCOME, ONCE AGAIN, TO THE FANTASTICAL UNDERWORLD OF **BROILERDOOM!** HERE, STRETCHED OUT BENEATH THE NIGHT SKY LIKE A SLUMBERING PREDATOR, LIES BROILERDOOM'S LARGEST HABITATION, **CORPSE CITY.**

AND, LIKE ANY TALENTED PREDATOR, THE CITY OFFERS A QUICK END FOR THOSE RESIDENTS FOOLISH ENOUGH TO DISTURB ITS REST.

AGGGHHHH!!! I'MSORRYI'MSORRY I'MSORRY!

NEXT!

BOOSH!

WE'RE RUNNING OUT OF STAFF, GENERAL. THAT WAS THE MINISTER FOR CAKES YOU JUST **FIRED.**

FIRED FROM A **CATAPULT** OFF THE **HIGHEST BALCONY OF MY PALACE!**, AND THE PUNISHMENT FITS THE CRIME, **VALUSH.** THAT HALFWIT BURNT MY BUNS.

HE BURNT YOUR—?

YES! BUT I DON'T WANT TO TALK ABOUT IT. NOW, SHOW IN THE NEXT VICTIM ... I MEAN, **CITIZEN.**

SECOND-IN-COMMAND AND HOW DO I SPEND MY DAYS? SCRAPING IDIOTS OFF THE PAVEMENT AND OPENING—

SALUTATIONS, YOUR UNDERWORLD-RULERNESS! MAY YOUR DAYS BE CREATIVE AND ENDLESS, AND YOUR CRUELTY BE ENDLESSLY CREATIVE!

SLAM!

SHUSH THAT NONSENSE AND SKIP TO THE PART WHERE YOU TELL ME **WHO** YOU ARE AND **WHAT** YOU WANT — AND IT HAD BETTER BE **INTERESTING!**

BONE-DRY HENSON, AT YOUR SERVICE, WITH A SIMPLE OFFER OF *REVENGE!* I HAVE THE MEANS TO RECAPTURE THE SLUMS FROM THOSE DO-GOODING *IRREGULARS!*

REGAIN CONTROL OF THE ENTIRE CITY? HMMM... INTERESTING! BUT WHAT IS THIS GOING TO *COST?*

OH, NOTHING YOU'D REGRET PARTING WITH. I WISH ONLY TO REPLACE ... *HIM.*

I BEG YOUR PARDON?

DEAL! BRING ME THE SLUMS AND COUNT VALUSH'S JOB IS *YOURS!* WHEN CAN YOU START?

WHY, MY DEAR GENERAL SPODE, 'THINGS' HAVE *ALREADY* BEGUN...

SNIFF

ACROSS THE CITY, OUR HEROES SLEEP PEACEFULLY BENEATH THE EVES OF **THE DEMON DRINK** - THAT MOST INFAMOUS OF TAVERNS, AND THE ONE PLACE THEY ALL CALL HOME.

REconstruction SITE. KEEP CLEAR!

0 6 5 DAYS SINCE LAST BATTLE.

...*Zz*n*Rrr*... ...I'LLTAKEYOUALLON... ...*zzzNz*...

...*zzzPuuuRrrzzz*... ...WHYCAN'TIGETAPONY?!... ...*Prrzzz*... ...WANTABIGPINKPONY...

LOST BOYS AND CRIMINAL CROWS **ONLY!** NO MONSTERS ALLOWED!

AFTER A STIRRING KICK IN THE HAMMOCK THE GANG ARE REUNITED ON THE STREET...

¡AY DIOS MÍO! THAT IS *NO* WAY TO ROUSE A DOZING CROW!

WHILE YOU WERE *SLEEPING,* CASTANET, YOUR BEST FRIEND WAS NEARLY SLICED IN TWO LIKE A HAM SANDWICH!

SORRY! BUT THIS GUARDIAN CROW BUSINESS IS NOT AS EASY AS IT LOOKS!

CLEAR A PATH! LARGE ANGRY DEMON AND TINY CONFUSED BOY COMING THROUGH!

EXCUSE ME, MADAM, BUT DID YOU *SEE* HIM?

SEE 'IM? OF COURSE I SAW 'IM! THING THAT SIZE IS 'ARD TO MISS!

WELL, DID ANYONE MANAGE TO CATCH HIM?

DOES OI LOOK LIKE OI'M MADE OF *GIANT TENTACLES,* YA CHEEKY BRAT!

I'M CONFUSED. AM I ASKING THE WRONG QUESTIONS?

NO, YOU JUST NEED TO ASK THE RIGHT ONE IN THE *RIGHT* MANNER.

WOULD YOU LIKE TO TRY A DIFFERENT ANSWER, RUNKLE?

Y-YES!! J-JUST S-STOP!!

SORRY ABOUT THAT! BUT WHAT HAPPENED TO THE STRANGER IN THE CLOAK?

OI DON'T KNOW ANY *STRANGER!* WE WAS DISCUSSIN' THE *WORM!*

WORM? YOU MEAN OUR PAL, THANATOS?

AY, THE GIANT MONSTER THAT HELPED YOU LOT SAVE THE SLUMS! THE MONSTER THAT'S RUMOURED TO CONTAIN SECRETS IN HIS BIG BELLY! GENERAL SPODE'S EVIL *MOAT* HAS SNARED HIM! SORRY, BUT... THE GREAT WORM IS *DEAD!*

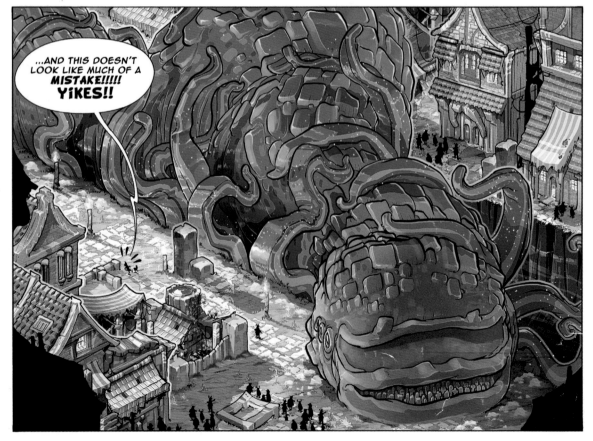

POOR, BRAVE THANATOS! HE SAVED THE **SLUMS** ONLY TO BE EATEN BY THE **CITY**!

AAA... AAA... AAAA...

SNIFF ... I'M TRYING NOT TO CRY TOO, BUDDY! BUT SOMETHING'S **WRONG.** LOOK AT THIS POWDER EVERYWHERE. IT FEELS A BIT LIKE—

AAA ... AAA... AAAA...

-CHOOO!!

WHOOPS! PARDON ME, DON! THAT COLD CAME ON **FAST**! AHA!

B-BLESS YOU, LITTLE C-CROW...

THANATOS!?!

YOU'RE STILL ALIVE!! WHAT HAPPENED? DID YOU FALL IN?

ALL THE S-SECRETS OF THE UNDERWORLD W-WILL BE YOURS IN GOOD TIME, DON ... **COUGH** ... BUT I'VE J-JUST **ONE** TO SHARE...

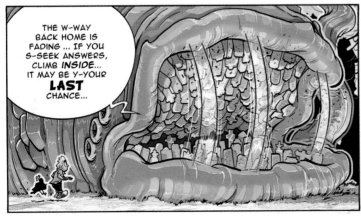

THE W-WAY BACK HOME IS FADING ... IF YOU S-SEEK ANSWERS, CLIMB **INSIDE**... IT MAY BE Y-YOUR **LAST** CHANCE...

IS **NOW** A GOOD TIME TO TELL YOU I'M ACTUALLY ALLERGIC TO **BEING EATEN!?**

I'M NOT GOING TO BE ABLE TO TALK YOU OUT OF THIS ONE, AM I?

NOPE! NOW, ARE YOU COMING?

...SIGH...

CHICO, I JUST HOPE THAT WHEN THE *YELLING* AND THE *SPRINTING* STARTS, YOU REMEMBER MY RELUCTANCE...

HOP!

ONLY IF YOU PROMISE NOT TO SAY "I TOLD YOU SO".

ARE YOU LOCO? CROWS DON'T MAKE PROMISES! BESIDES, THAT'S MY FAVOURITE LINE.

LOOK AT THE WRITING ON THESE TOMBSTONES: 'HERE LIES OTKAR RIBSPLITTER, – "THE EVER-LIVING TROLL" – WHO, IRONICALLY, WAS A FIBBER, AS HE WAS SKEWED BY A POLE.'

EVEN BY GENERAL SPODE'S STANDARDS, OLD OTKAR WAS *NASTY!* ONLY ATE FOOD THAT COULD TALK.

IF YOU KNEW OTKAR, THAT MEANS THESE GRAVES ARE REAL ...

THEY'RE REALLY REAL GRAVES!!

WELL, WHAT DID *YOU* THINK THEY WERE DOING HERE?

I DON'T KNOW... I GUESSED... **DECORATION** OR **GRAFFITI** OR SOMETHING!

THEY'RE REAL ALL RIGHT, WHICH MEANS SOMEONE PUT THEM HERE. I CAN'T IMAGINE ANYONE *MAD* ENOUGH TO TAKE THAT JOB!

WHAT, HERE, IN BROILERDOOM? I CAN THINK OF A FEW — WAIT, DO YOU HEAR THAT?

TAKK! TOK! TIK!

SWEET SARCOPHAGUS! THAT IS ONE *BIG* TOMBSTONE!

RETREEEAT! RETREEEAT!

YES! BRILLIANTLY **GROSS!** YOU SCARED THEM OFF **AND** TAUGHT THEM A NEW WORD!

THERE'S NOT A LOT I DON'T KNOW ABOUT THE INNER WORKINGS OF MY MASTER!

BLURRRGH! DO YOU KNOW HOW IT FEELS TO BE G-GARGLED LIKE M-MONSTER MOUTHWASH?!

YES I DO. NOW, LET'S SEE ABOUT FINDING THE *HEART OF* THANTOS'S SICKNESS!

CHEER UP, BUDDY. LOOK WHAT *I* MANAGED TO RESCUE!

MY SOMBRERO! THAT ACTUALLY IS GOOD NEWS! BUT NEXT TIME, *YOU* RIDE THE ROLLERCOASTER!

THE REST OF THE JOURNEY PASSES WITHOUT INCIDENT...

IF YOU THINK THIS IS CONNECTED TO THE PORTAL, THEN THAT MEANS ENTERING *THE HALL OF MUNCHING...*

HWUH-?!

DID WE TAKE A WRONG TURN, TONTO? THERE'S NO PORTAL HERE...

WELL, SOMETHING **MUCHO** BIG WAS RESTING ON THIS CUSHION. AND THERE'S MORE OF THAT WEIRD *POWDER* WE FOUND OUTSIDE...

THE H-H-H-H...!! THE H-H-H-H...!!

WHAT'S THE MATTER, TONTO?

THE **HEART!** IT'S **GONE!** SOMEONE'S STOLEN THE **HEART OF THANATOS!**

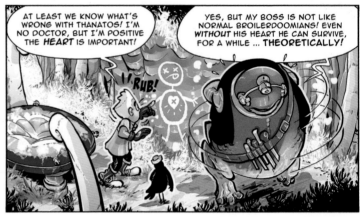

YOU GO WITH THE YOUNG LADY. I'M GOING TO STAY WITH THE BOSS...

WE'LL FIND HIS HEART, TONTO! AND THAT'S A **PROMISE!**

I *REALLY* HOPE THIS IS IMPORTANT, SAFINA.

I WOULDN'T DRAG YOU FROM HELPING YOUR FRIEND IF I WASN'T *SERIOUSLY* WORRIED!

SAFINA LEADS THE TRIO THROUGH THE SLUMS, WHERE ALL IS NOT WELL. IN FACT, ALL APPEARS TO BE EXTREMELY STRANGE...

WHO WANTS TO SEE ME EAT MY OWN **FEET?!**

PENNY FOR THE DANCER?

?!

I'M JUGGLING FIRE! AND IT *REALLY* HURTS! HOHO! BUT I'M LAUGHING!!

AUDIENCE

SEVERAL THOUSAND LOONIES LATER, THE TRIO APPROACH THEIR HOME, **THE DEMON DRINK**...

WHAT'S GOING ON? THE UNDERWORLD'S A STRANGE PLACE BUT THIS IS *WEIRD!* EVERYONE'S ACTING COMPLETELY CRAZY!

CRAZY IS WHAT WE DO BEST.

NOT LIKE THIS! AND IT GETS MUCH WORSE!

NGGN ... OH, THANK GOODNESS! I THOUGHT YOU WERE NEVER COMING BACK!

HOW ARE THE PATIENTS, RIPLEY?

UNTIL HE DECIDED I WAS A BUFFALO TO BE HUNTED, I'D HAVE SAID THINGS WERE GOING QUITE WELL. FOR A HARMLESS SOUL, VIKTOR'S BECOME RATHER **VIOLENT!**

POP!

I DON'T EVEN KNOW WHAT A "BUFFALO" IS...

TO THE LIBRARY

HA! THAT'S *JUST* WHAT A BUFFALO WOULD SAY!

VIKTOR? HAVE YOU BUILT A *FORT* FROM PILES OF YOUR PRICELESS BOOKS?

YOU NEED A STURDY BASE TO REPEL SNEAKY COWBOY ATTACKS! BUT *WHY* IS THAT BUFFALO STILL *ROAMING?!*

THAT 'BUFFALO' IS *RIPLEY!* THE MAYOR OF THE SLUMS, AND YOUR *FRIEND!* PLUS, IT WAS THE *COWBOYS* WHO LIVED IN FORTS.

HOW DARE YOU?! I'M NOT A COWBOY! I'M THE GREAT CHIEF, **WOBBLY BOBBLE!** AND THIS IS MY FEARLESS STEED, **SPLASHY!**

WELL, APART FROM THE ANGER, NOTHING SEEMS OUT OF ORDER HERE. 'ODD' IS NORMAL FOR VIKTOR.

MAY I HANG UP YOUR SOMBRERO, SIR?

MUCHOS GRACIAS, COMPADRE. KEEP A CLOSE EYE ON IT.

YOUR HEADWEAR WILL NEVER BE FAR FROM MY THOUGHTS, SIR.

!?!

ANOTHER BUFFALO! THE TRIBE WILL EAT WELL TONIGHT!

OH, JOLLY GOOD SHOT, SIR!

PONK!

SAFINA?! HELP!

LET'S GO UPSTAIRS. CASTANET, STAY AND GIVE RIPLEY A HAND!

DON'T LEAVE ME WITH THESE GUYS! I WON'T SURVIVE FIVE MINUTES!!

TWANG!

OW!!

BULLSEYE, SIR! ER, I MEAN, *BIRDS* EYE.

THEY WERE BOTH FINE EARLIER ... I DON'T UNDERSTAND WHAT'S HAPPENING.

YOU KNOW MORE THAN YOU REALISE, DON. AND VIKTOR *WASN'T* FINE.

HE THOUGHT HE'D LOST HIS *RUBBER DUCK*, REMEMBER?

OH, YEAH. HE WAS REALLY UPSET ABOUT IT.

THAT DUCK WAS HIS **TOTEM** – IT WAS HIS *ONLY* CONNECTION TO HIS OWN WORLD. JUST LIKE YOUR SCHOOL TIE. YOU *DO* STILL HAVE THE TIE?

ALWAYS! BUT I THOUGHT LOSING YOUR PRECIOUS TOTEM JUST ROBBED YOU OF YOUR MEMORIES OF HOME.

THAT DEPENDS ON HOW *LONG* YOU'VE BEEN STUCK HERE. HAVING MISPLACED THEIR TOTEMS, VIKTOR, LEWD AND THE OLDER CITIZENS OUTSIDE HAVE NOW LOST THEIR *MINDS!* THEIR PERSONALITIES ARE FLIPPING – FROM HAPPY TO SAD; FROM MEAK TO **MENTAL!**

WHOA ... WHAT DID *LEWD* LOSE?

HIS WAISTCOAT. BUT I DON'T BELIEVE IT'S LOST. I THINK IT'S ALL BEEN **STOLEN**, AND BY THE SAME FIEND WE CAUGHT IN YOUR ROOM. HE WAS THERE TO SWIPE *YOUR* TOTEM! JUST LOOK AT THIS...

LAST WEEK I HEARD A RUMOUR THAT A NEW GANG OF THIEVES HAD BEGUN WORKING IN THE CITY. I DON'T LIKE *COMPETITION* SO DECIDED TO LOOK THEM OVER. I GOT A LOOK ... AND IT WAS *NOT* GOOD!

?!?

WHAT... WHAT IS IT? WHERE ARE ITS *EYES?*

SCARY, RIGHT, AND I'M CONVINCED THAT *THIS* GUY AND HIS GANG ARE RESPONSIBLE FOR THE MISSING TOTEMS! NOW, THERE'S NOTHING WE CAN DO TONIGHT, SO LET'S GET SOME REST, AND JUST *HOPE* THAT THINGS LOOK BETTER IN THE MORNING...

BUT THE EARLY SUN DOES LITTLE TO COOL THE SLUMS. AS THE NEW DAY DAWNS, TEMPERS AND TEMPERATURES CONTINUE TO RISE...

CROCK-A-HOOODEE-WOOOOO!

WILL YOU GIVE IT A BREAK?!

I'M THE ROOSTER 'ROUND HERE! AND IT'S 'COCK-A-DOODLE-*DOOOOO*'!

HOOP-DA-BOOBLY-ROOOO!!

AND, OUTSIDE **THE DEMON DRINK...**

YAWWWN! CROWING AND NOW *BANGING!* DIDN'T RECONSTRUCTION STOP WHEN THE WORKFORCE WENT MAD?

BANG! BONG! BANG!

IT'S NOT THE BUILDERS, CASTANET - IT'S *RIPLEY.*

BANG! BAM! BANG! BONG

INDEED IT IS! THE SLUMS ARE BEING TORN APART BY MADNESS AND AS MAYOR, IT'S HIGH TIME I TOOK CHARGE! *FIRM ACTION* IS REQUIRED, SEE?

ATTENTION LUNATICS! YOUR PRESENCE IS REQUIRED AT A SPECIAL COUNCIL MEETING: TODAY!! (FREE TEA AND BISCUITS FOR ALL!) MEETING TO BE FOLLOWED BY RAFFLE! GREAT PRIZES TO BE WON!

STRONG STUFF, EH?

OOOOH, THIS IS GOING TO BE *GOOD!*

AND LATER, ENCOURAGED BY THE PROMISE OF A HOT DRINK, THE RECENTLY INSANE SLUM POPULATION GATHER IN THE COURTYARD OF ARCH HALL.

OW!! ...HEHEHE... STOP HITTING MY ...HAHAHA... FUNNY BONE!!

WHAM! WALLOP! THUMP!

COUNCIL MEETING! FREE BISCUITS FOR A

ARE YOU SMILING?!

YES. NO. WELL, MAYBE A LITTLE!

BANG! WHOMP! CRASH!

NO ONE'S LISTENING TO ME! JUST LOOK AT THIS MESS ... THE CITIZENS ARE REVOLTING!

SOME OF THEM CERTAINLY ARE...

BAM!

COCK-A-WOOBLY SNOOOOOO!

BOP! WHUMP!

AND I SAY TO YOU, MADAM, THAT A BRICK IS A MUCH BETTER PET THAN A BOWL OF WATER!

BONK!

ENOUGH! I'M GETTING MY PICTURE OF THAT WEIRD THIEF. THE ONLY WAY RIPLEY'S GOING TO STOP THIS MAYHEM IS BY FINDING OUT WHO'S LEADING THAT GANG AND WHY!

WHAT EXACTLY ARE THEY FIGHTING ABOUT?

ANYTHING... EVERYTHING... AND NOTHING AT ALL...

ISN'T SORTING THIS OUT A JOB FOR THE SLUM GUARDS?

WELL, YOU CAN ASK THEM IF YOU LIKE. THEY'RE JUST ABOUT TO ... SIGH ... PERFORM.

PERFORM?

27

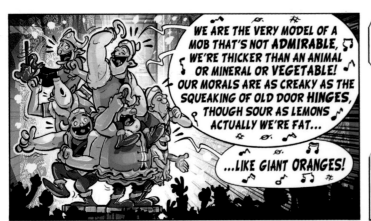

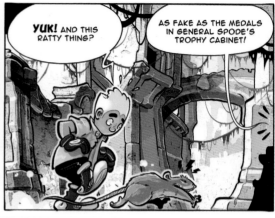

SEE, I TOLD YOU I WAS UNTOUCHABLE.

THAT PROTECTION APPLIES TO MY GRUBBY UNDERLINGS, CASTANET, NOT **YOU**!

COME ON, **JUJU**, YOU WOULDN'T HURT YOUR OWN FAMILY!

REALLY? MAY I REMIND YOU THAT THE WORD TO DESCRIBE A GROUP OF CROWS IS A **"MURDER"**!

WHOA!! WE'RE ONLY HERE TO HELP A FRIEND, NOT TO ARGUE! LET'S NOT GET OVER EXCITED...

WHY NOT? IT'S **HIS** STINKING FAULT WE'RE IN THIS MESS!

ONE LITTLE MISTAKE AND YOU NEVER HEAR THE END OF IT...

HUGGING MY WINGS WHILE REFUSING TO FLY YOURSELF, ISN'T A **"LITTLE MISTAKE"** WHEN WE'RE FORTY FEET UP!!

I SENSE YOU HAVE A GOOD HEART, PAL, BUT THIS UNDERWORLD DOESN'T LIKE **HEROES** OR **SAINTS**, WHICH IS WHY I SPEND MY DAYS HANGING RIVALS UP BY THEIR EARS.

WHAT LIES! JUJU'S ALWAYS BEEN A BULLY, DON! HE USED TO PAINT ME WHITE AND TELL THE LOCAL FLOCK I WAS A PIGEON!

I WAS DRINKING THAT!

GLUG! GLUG!

DON'T YOU GO CRYING **FOWL**, BIRDBRAIN!

HEY, YOU'VE **RUFFLED A A LOT MORE FEATHERS** THAN ME!!

WHY NOT? **TOUCAN PLAY AT THATGAME!**

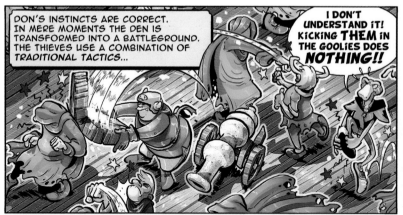

WAAA-HA HAHAHA!

TICKLE! TICKLE!

THOSE CRUEL SWINE! HOW COULD THEY LEAVE HER *HERE*!

WHAT *IS* THAT THING? AND WHAT'S IT DOING TO SAFINA?

BROTHER, YOUR LACK OF LOCAL KNOWLEDGE IS SHOCKING! DON'T YOU RECOGNISE A *TICKLEUMP* WHEN YOU SEE ONE?!

ARMS AS WEAK AS A KITTEN'S TAIL, BUT THERE'S *NO* DEFENCE AGAINST THOSE *FEATHERY FINGERS*...

GEDDOFFFAME!! HEHEHEHE!

LAUGHING YOURSELF INTO A GRAVE ... NASTY WAY FOR SUCH A PRETTY THIEF TO MEET HER END!

AT LEAST SHE'LL GO WITH A SMILE ON HER FACE.

HMM...

NOBODY IS DYING TODAY! I'VE A CUNNING PLAN, BUT IT'S GOING TO REQUIRE FEARLESS HEROICS AND PERFECT TIMING!

WHAT A PITY! THOSE ARE *JUST* THE ITEMS I FORGOT TO PACK!

AND SO...

HEY, YOU BIG FEATHERED FIEND! TRY TICKLING SOMETHING THAT CAN *TICKLE BACK*!

?

GAHAHA!

UM ... YOU'RE NOT BRINGING **THAT** WITH US?!

IT'S FAR TOO DANGEROUS TO LEAVE RUNNING WILD, CAS!

AGREED! LEWD USED TO LIVE IN THE **MARSHES**, BACK WHEN HE WAS A RANGER. HE'LL BE ABLE TO TAKE CARE OF IT.

QUEEN THIEF, MAY I ESCORT YOU AND YOUR CARGO TO THE SLUMS?

THANK YOU, DEAR JUJU! YOUR COMPANY WOULD BE MUCH APPRECIATED.

PAT PAT

THE STRANGE PROCESSION SETS OFF...

FIRST THE HEART OF THANATOS GOES MISSING, THEN THE ENTIRE SLUMS GO **MAD!** AND LET'S NOT FORGET THE GANG OF FACELESS CROOKS TRYING TO KILL US ALL! IT DOESN'T MAKE ANY SENSE!

BEFORE THOSE BOZOS LEFT ME HERE I DISCOVERED THEIR **SECRET!**

THEY TRIED TO FIND **MY** TOTEM, THIS **NECKLACE!** THESE ARE THE CHUMPS THAT HAVE STOLEN EVERY SINGLE MISSING THING!

BUT TOTEMS JUST STOP US FROM LOSING OUR MINDS! WHAT COULD BE GAINED FROM A CITY FULL OF **LOONIES?**

BACK AT **ARCH HALL**, A FRUSTRATED RIPLEY IS ABOUT TO DISCOVER THE ANSWER TO THAT VERY QUESTION...

CALL THAT A **CONGA LINE?!** I'VE SEEN BETTER DANCING AT THE END OF A **HANGMAN'S ROPE!**

THEY'RE ALL COMPLETELY **DOOLALLY!**

SIR, THERE'S A **SKELETON** AT THE DOOR WHO'D LIKE A WORD. HE APPEARS TO BE ACCOMPANIED BY A SMALL **ARMY**. SHALL I LAY OUT THE FINE CHINA?

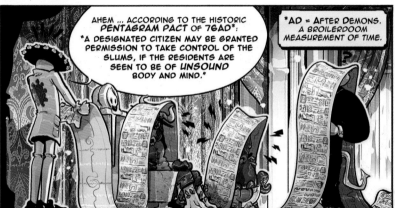

LATER THAT DAY...

PUFF ... WHY DID IT TAKE US SO MUCH *LONGER* TO GET OUT OF THE SWAMP?

HMM? DID IT? I HADN'T NOTICED...

BUT THEN ... *SIGH* ... I'VE HAD OTHER THINGS ON MY MIND...

A LOVESICK CRIMINAL MASTERMIND! *JUST* WHAT THIS CITY NEEDS!

ACTUALLY, I THINK THE CITY HAS *BIGGER* PROBLEMS THAN DEAR JUJU...

WELCOME TO BONE-DRY-BURG

LAND OF THE ENSLAVED! HOME OF THE INSANE!

?!?

HENSON IS... WATCHING YOU!!

IT'S ... IT'S THOSE CRAZY FACELESS ODDBALLS! THEY'RE *EVERYWHERE!*

THAT'S HOW THEY MANAGED TO PINCH EVERYONE'S TOTEMS. IT'S NOT A SMALL GANG OF THIEVES...

...IT'S AN *ARMY OF CROOKS!!!* AND THEY'VE STOLEN OUR SLUMS!

HERE TO HELP!

UNDER NEW MANAGEMENT

OKAY, THIS IS *REALLY* BAD! WE NEED TO FIND RIPLEY—

OH, BUT YOU *HAVE.*

DEAR RIPLEY HAS RESIGNED. *MY* NAME IS *HENSON* AND I'M YOUR NEW MAYOR. THERE'S GOING TO BE SOME CHANGES AROUND HERE ... *NONE* OF WHICH YOU'LL ENJOY! HEHE!

AND SO, HENSON'S REIGN OF EVIL DESCENDS UPON AN UNSUSPECTING CITY.

SPLAT!

WITH THE MYSTERIOUS FACELESS ENEMY NOW IN CHARGE, THE FUTURE OF THE SLUMS LOOKS MOST UNCERTAIN.

?!

BUT KINGDOMS THAT ARE TAKEN INSTEAD OF EARNED ARE RATHER LIKE A BADLY MADE CAKE. WHILE THEY MIGHT RISE IN THE BEGINNING...

...EVENTUALLY THEY ALL CRUMBLE AND FALL!

SPLOOOGE!

AMAZING! WHAT A SHOT!

I TOLD YOU, CHICO, IT'S ALL IN THE WING.

YOU MIGHT HAVE OVER-EGGED THAT LAST ROUND.

OVER-EGGED! NEVER!

AN EGG IN THE FACE NEVER HURT ANYONE ... PERHAPS WITH THE EXCEPTION OF YOU AND YOUR HORRIBLY LOW SCORE!

DON CAST.

THIS UNDERWORLD IS A STRANGE AND DANGEROUS PLACE, DON, BUT EVERY ONCE IN A WHILE IT CAN BE IMMENSELY PLEASURABLE!

HUMPH ... I'M NOT SURE THIS IS ONE OF THOSE TIMES, BUDDY...

HAS EVERYONE MET OUR FRIEND, TONTO?

YES. THE POOR THING HASN'T STOPPED CRYING SINCE HE GOT HERE. MUST HAVE BEEN HARD TO LEAVE THANATOS IN THE MOAT.

BRUSH!

BRUSH!

WELL, WE'VE HIT THE GUARD DOWNSTAIRS WITH HUNDREDS OF EGGS, BUT HE HASN'T MOVED, LET ALONE CRIED! HE DOESN'T EVEN DUCK!

A SOLDIER WHO TAKES AN OMELETTE IN THE FACE EVERY DAY FOR A WEEK IS DOWNRIGHT PECULIAR.

BRUSH!

BRUSH!

BRUSH!

IT'S MUCH WORSE THAN THAT, SAFINA. IT'S UNNATURAL!

WHAT, LIKE THIS TICKLEUMP, RIPLEY?

NOT AT ALL! THIS CREATURE IS VERY MUCH A PART OF BROILERDOOM!

HIS FEATHERS FOR INSTANCE — THEY'RE SUPPOSED TO BE RUFFLED AND YET I JUST CAN'T HELP BUT TIDY HIM UP! I NURTURE WHEN I'M NERVOUS!

EVERYONE ARRIVES IN BROILERDOOM ALONE, LIKE YOU DID, DON. ONCE IN A WHILE THEY MIGHT APPEAR IN TWOS LIKE CASTANET AND JUJU. BUT HENSON'S SOLDIERS APPEARED OVERNIGHT IN THEIR HUNDREDS!

SOB ... I J-JUST WISH THEY'D RETURN POOR THANATOS'S H-HEART! MY MASTER IS R-RUNNING OUT OF T-TIME!

HE'S NOT THE ONLY ONE. GREETINGS, BUFFOONS! MIND IF I CRASH YOU PARTY?

COUNT VALUSH!!

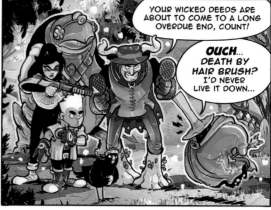

LATER, THE **BRIDGE OF CROSSING** – THE PATHWAY SEPARATING THE SLUMS FROM CORPSE CITY...

YOU IMBECILES! DO YOU KNOW WHO YOU'RE DEALING WITH?

COURSE! YOU BE *COUNT VALUSH*. AT LEAST I FINK YOU ARE...

IT'S NOT DAT WE DON'T TRUST YOU! IT'S JUST, WELL... YOU SEEM A BIT **"DIFFERENT"**.

WHY ARE YOU WALKING ABOUT? ... AH – I MEAN, **WHAT ARE YOU TALKING ABOUT?!**

WHEN YOU LEFT THE CITY EARLIER, YOU WERE A LITTLE LESS... UM ... WHAT'S THE WORD I'M FINKING OF, ELMO?

FAT?

HOW DARE YOU?

I'VE NEVER BEEN SO INSULTED IN MY LIFE! GET OUT OF MY WAY BEFORE I THROW YOU IN THE MOAT!

PHEW! DAT WAS A NEAR MISS!

YOU'RE TELLING ME... BUT YOU KNOW, THE WORD I WAS FINKING OF WAS *'LEGGY'*...

THE PECULIAR SHAPE OF COUNT VALUSH TOTTERS THROUGH THE STREETS OF CORPSE CITY, UNTIL FINALLY...

OKAY, OUT YOU COME.

GAH! **N–NEVER AGAIN!!** WHAT ... WHAT ARE YOU MADE OF VALUSH?!

THIS PARROT TRICK COMES IN HANDY, DON! I DIDN'T SEE A THING!

OPEN YOUR EYES, BEAKY, AND BEHOLD... **HENSON'S SMELTING WORKS!!**

HENSON'S

IT'S A BONE DRY BUSINESS

KEEP OUT!

POISON!

DANGER!

WHOA – THAT'S **SCARY!!!**

48

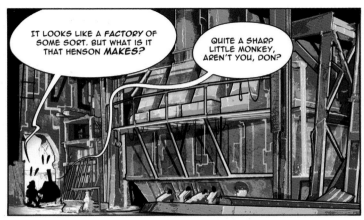

WE CAN'T OUTRUN A TIDAL WAVE! LET'S HEAD FOR HIGH GROUND!

AGH! NOT AGAIN!

WOULD IT HELP IF WE APOLOGISED FOR MELTING THEIR FRIENDS?!

ONLY IF YOU MEANT IT. AND I'M NOT IN THE LEAST BIT SORRY.

ET VOILÀ! MORONS BEGONE.

SWIIIIIIING!

KRASSH!

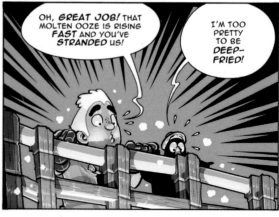

OH, GREAT JOB! THAT MOLTEN OOZE IS RISING FAST AND YOU'VE STRANDED US!

I'M TOO PRETTY TO BE DEEP-FRIED!

WHERE ARE WE SUPPOSED TO GO NOW, VALUSH?!

AH. RIGHT. WE'LL BE DOOMED THEN...

EXIT

THINK ... THINK *FAST* ... WE NEED SOMETHING TO BRIDGE THAT GAP!

A SIGN LIKE THAT WOULD BE PERFECT IF WE COULD REACH THE CHAINS.

FIGHT HARD & BE MEAN TO PEOPLE

YOU'RE RIGHT ... SO GIVE ME YOUR SWORD, VALUSH. I'M GOING TO MAKE A STRAP FOR IT WITH MY SCHOOL TIE!

I'VE A *REALLY* BIG FAVOUR TO ASK, CAS! WE NEED YOUR WINGS.

MY *WINGS?!* O-OKAY. I'LL TRY! BUT DON'T HOLD YOUR BREATH...

I'M A LEAF ON THE WIND! I'M A LEAF ON THE WIND! ...NNNGNN...

FLAP!

NNGGN!!

FLAP! FLAP! FLAP!

YOU'RE FLYING, CASTANET! REALLY *FLYING!!* JUST A LITTLE HIGHER!

GAH! I ... I MADE IT!

WOO HOO! WHO SAYS YOU CAN'T TEACH AN OLD CROW NEW TRICKS?

YEAH - TAKE *THAT*, INANIMATE OBJECT!

SHINK!

CHIING!

YAAAAAAAAAH!

WHHJJP!

HEY, WAIT FOR US, CASTANET!

I'M NOT SURE I LIKE THIS NEW *EAGER* SIDE OF YOUR FRIEND. I PREFER MY ENEMIES A LITTLE MORE—

YOU'D ARREST THE WHOLE TOWN, HENSON, JUST TO GET THE JOB AS SPODE'S LAP DOG?

COURSE NOT! I INTEND TO **DESTROY** OLD SPODEY AND BECOME **LORD OF BROILERDOOM!**

BUT I NEEDED EVERYONE LIKELY TO SPOIL MY SCHEME UNDER LOCK AND KEY! I TOOK THE SLUMS, THEN YOU IRREGULARS, AND NOW I'LL TAKE THE **WHOLE CITY!**

I DON'T CARE ABOUT THAT — JUST ADMIT IT! **YOU STOLE MY FRIEND'S HEART!**

WHAT? YOUR PARROT IS IN **LOVE** WITH ME?

THE NERVE OF THIS CLOWN... I'M A **CROW!!**

YOU'RE TALKING ABOUT **THANATOS!** YES, GUILTY AS CHARGED, BUT HOW DID YOU WORK THAT OUT?

I **JUST** SOLVED IT! THE PILES OF **WHITE POWDER** AT THE SCENE OF THE CRIME — THEY'RE THE REMAINS OF YOUR **SOLDIERS!**

BOINK!

CLEVER BRAT! AS THE LAST IN A LINE OF **UNDEAD POTTERS** I POSSESS THE POWER TO BRING CLAY TO LIFE. BUT MY UNDERLINGS HAVE ALWAYS BEEN ... FRAGILE!

THE ISSUE IS THAT HENCHMEN LACK BOTH **HEART** AND **POWER!** TWO PROBLEMS I'VE SOLVED WITH ONE BIG STONE...

TUMP! THUMP! THUMP! THUMP!

ALLOW ME TO INTRODUCE **TERROR-COTTA!** MY GREATEST CREATION, WITH THE STRENGTH OF A **GOD** THANKS TO HIS NEW MONSTER HEART!

LOOK! THAT BIG BRUTE'S SAVED THE TOTEMS FROM THE FACTORY!

TOTEMS

IF THOSE TRINKETS MEAN SO MUCH, DON, THEY'RE YOURS ... IF YOU CAN SURVIVE A **DUEL** AGAINST MY NEW CHAMPION!

A D-D-DUEL? WITH THAT THING? I CAN'T ... I CAN'T...

AGREED! YOU'RE MORE LIKELY TO CHEWING THROUGH THESE BARS! **NOM NOM!** UGH ... THIS CAGE NEEDS **FLAVOUR...**

DESPITE CASTANET'S BEST EFFORTS OUR HEROES FAIL TO ESCAPE AND THE HOUR OF THE DUEL APPROACHES...

WHAT IS THE MEANING OF THIS **NONSENSE?!**

ENSLAVED CITIZENS! THIS WAY FOR THE BIG SHOW!

HENSON, **WHY** IS MY FAVOURITE DEATH ARENA FULL OF GRUBBY AND UNATTRACTIVE PEASANTS?!

TAKE **HEART**, GENERAL. ALL THE ANSWERS ARE COMING.

SHACKLED SLUM DWELLERS! YOU STAND HERE TODAY AS TESTAMENT TO THE SUCCESS OF MY LEADERSHIP!

WITHOUT RESORTING TO VIOLENCE I HAVE DESTROYED YOUR SANITY AND WON YOUR DRIBBLING OBEDIENCE...

WHAT'S THAT NUMBSKULL BLITHERING ON ABOUT!

MISTER HENSON IS GIVING A "HEARTS AND MINDS" SPEECH, SIR.

IF ANYONE'S STILL FEELING *REBELLIOUS*, I'VE ARRANGED A LITTLE DEMONSTRATION OF MY **TRUE** POWER!

LOOK ... LOOK! IT'S DON!

GAH!!

GULP ... MY BIGGEST F-FEAR USED TO BE OUR NEIGHBOURS' *DOG!* HOW TIMES CHANGE!